Hutterites
in Canada

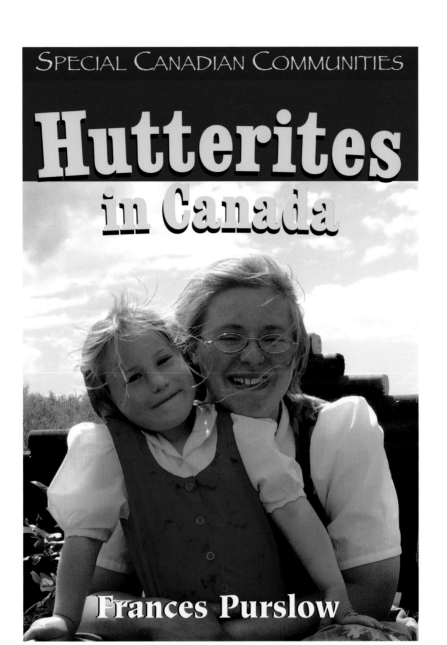

Frances Purslow

Weigl
CALGARY

Published by Weigl Educational Publishers Limited
6325-10 Street SE
Calgary, Alberta
Canada T2H 2Z9
Web site: www.weigl.ca

All of the Internet URLs given in the book were valid at the time of publication. However, due to the
dynamic nature of the Internet, some addresses may have changed, or sites may have ceased to exist
since publication. While the author and publisher regret any inconvenience this may cause readers,
no responsibility for any such changes can be accepted by either the author or the publisher.

Library and Archives Canada Cataloguing in Publication Data

Purslow, Frances
        The Hutterites in Canada / Frances Purslow.

(Special Canadian communities)
Includes index.
ISBN 1-55388-098-6 (bound).--ISBN 1-55388-111-7 (pbk.)

        1. Hutterite Brethren--Canada--Juvenile literature.
2. Hutterite Brethren--Canada--History--Juvenile literature.
I. Title. II. Series: Special Canadian communities (Calgary, Alta.)

FC106.H97P87 2005   j971'.0088'28973   C2004-907475-X

Printed and bound in China
1 2 3 4 5 6 7 8 9 0   09 08 07 06 05

Photograph Credits
Every reasonable effort has been made to trace ownership and to obtain permission to reprint
copyright material. The publishers would be pleased to have any errors or omissions brought
to their attention so that they may be corrected in subsequent printings.

Cover: Hutterite women work on colonies as cooks, gardeners, teachers, and seamstresses. Girls help
with chores.

Cover: George Webber Photography; **Jeff Brown:** page 5; **Calgary Herald:** page 10 (Bill Herriot);
Corel Corporation: page 4B; **Clipart.com:** page 4T; **Decker Colony:** pages 1, 3BM, 3B, 8T, 8B, 9B,
12T, 14B, 15, 18B, 20, 22T, 22B, 23TR; **Glenbow Museum:** page 14T (NA-3193-1); **Carol Koopmans:**
pages 7, 11, 12B, 13, 16B, 19; **Library and Archives Canada:** pages 6 (C-036153), 23TL (C-036153);
Photos.com: pages 3T, 3TM, 9T, 16T, 17, 18T, 23B.

Project Coordinator Heather C. Hudak **Design** Warren Clark **Layout** Kathryn Livingstone and
Jeff Brown **Copy Editor** Janice L. Redlin **Photo Research** Kim Winiski **Consultant** Rosebud
Colony and Andy Wipf, Lakeside Colony, Alberta **Researcher** Carol Koopmans

We acknowledge the financial support of the Government of Canada through the Book Publishing
Industry Development Program (BPIDP) for our publishing activities.

Contents

Coming to Canada 4

Hutterite Communities 6

Celebrating Culture 8

Learning German Language 10

Communal Culture 12

Songs of Praise 14

Farm Fresh Foods 16

Cultural Contributions 18

Further Research 20

Hearts, Flowers, and Dandy Designs 21

What Have You Learned? 22

Glossary/Index 24

Coming to Canada

Hutterites are a religious group. They helped create large farming communities in parts of Canada. Hutterite **culture** began in 1528 in Moravia. This area is now known as the Czech Republic. The Czech Republic is a country in central Europe. Jakob Hutter led this first Hutterite group. This is why they are called Hutterites.

Many countries did not accept the Hutterite religion. The Hutterites moved many times to escape being treated poorly. They moved to Hungary, then Romania and Russia. These countries are in eastern Europe. In the 1870s, they moved to North and South Dakota in the United States.

Hutterites are a peaceful people. Many countries did not agree with their beliefs. They had to flee these countries to avoid fighting in wars. Hutterites did not want to fight in World War I. They moved to Canada, where they could choose not to go to war.

Czech Republic

Germany borders the Czech Republic on the north and west. Austria is south of the Czech Republic. Slovakia is southeast of the Czech Republic, while Poland is northeast.

Think About It

Can you find Austria, Germany, the Czech Republic, Slovakia, and Poland on the map? What part of the world does your family come from? At the library, find a map of this country. Where is it located?

Hutterite Communities

Between 1914 and 1918, many Canadian men were soldiers in World War I. There were too few men to work on farms in the western provinces. Hutterites were known for their hard work. They also had very good farming methods. The first large group of Hutterites came to Canada from South Dakota in 1918.

Three Hutterite groups settled in different parts of Canada. Schmiedeleut settled in Manitoba. Dariusleut settled in Saskatchewan, Alberta, and British Columbia. Lehrerleut settled in Saskatchewan and Alberta.

Today, there are more than 36,000 Hutterites in North America. They live on 469 **colonies**. The prairie provinces are home to 335 colonies. Hutterites are farmers, so they live where there is good farmland.

In 1918, Hutterites began moving from North Dakota and South Dakota to Alberta and Manitoba.

Hutterite History

"Being a Hutterite is different than being another person. With three languages, we can communicate better. We can switch from one language to another without even thinking about it. It is sometimes easier to talk with one language than it is with another. It makes you feel important. It is a challenge. Our languages connect us to our history and our **tradition**. Tradition is important because we do not want to upset our **ancestors**. Even though they are dead, the preachers are not. The preacher reminds us to keep our tradition. The English world is different, not better or worse. We are lucky to have such a culture and language."

■ By 1940, there were fifty-two Hutterite colonies in Canada.

Think About It

Imagine it is the early 1900s. You have just arrived in Canada from South Dakota. How has your life changed? Write a letter to family members in South Dakota. Tell them about your trip and new life in Canada.

Celebrating Culture

Hutterites live together in colonies. They share and help each other. Hutterites work together as a team or a large family. They know that many people working together can make a big job easier.

Hutterites brought their cultural traditions to Canada. These traditions include their religion, language, food, clothing, colony lifestyle, and farming methods. Traditions are passed down to younger generations.

All Hutterite celebrations are based on their religion. The most important event is when a Hutterite child becomes an adult. Most Hutterite children finish school when they are 15 or 16 years of age. They work in the colony. Hutterite children also attend religion classes. At about 20 years old, they are **baptized**. Then, they are adults.

Harvest Party

ost Hutterite colonies have **harvest** parties called *Hapchincka*. Hapchincka is a Russian word meaning "celebrating the bountiful harvest." On the first Sunday after all of the crops are harvested, Hutterites have a special dinner. The meal might include breaded shrimp, spareribs, and hot wings. Sometimes, Hutterites invite friends and neighbours who do not live on the colony to join them. It is an evening of food, friends, fun, and song.

■ Most Hutterite colonies farm about 1.2 hectares of land. They grow wheat, barley, oats, and canola. Some also grow corn, soybeans, peas, radishes, and flax.

■ Hutterite children help their parents with many farm chores.

Think About It

What special holidays does your family celebrate? Think about these celebrations. Do any events, colours, or foods have special meanings?

Learning German Language

Hutterites speak the German language in their homes and the colony. They speak a special **dialect** of German. When Hutterite children begin school at 5 or 6 years of age, they learn English. At school, they also learn "High German." All church services are spoken in High German. Hutterites can speak all three languages very well.

Families speak Hutterite German when talking to each other. They speak English when talking to people who do not live on the colony.

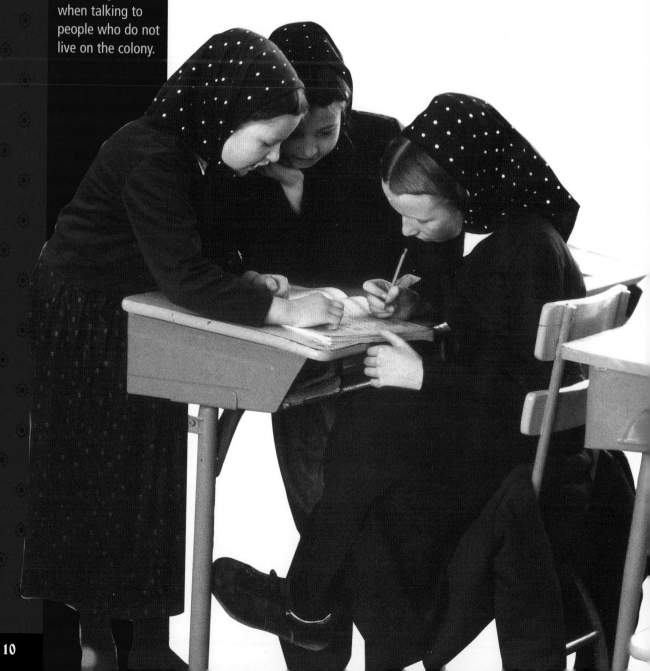

Learning the Language

Try saying some of the following words and phrases.

English	German
hello	Hallo, or Guten Tag
goodbye	Auf Wiedersehen
How are you?	Wie Geht's?
thank you	Danke
please	Bitte
people	Leute
colony	Bruderhof

All traditional Hutterite religious books and prayers are written in German.

Think About It

Try practising these German words. How do they compare to the English language? Do you speak any other languages? Try writing these words in your language, too.

Communal Culture

AHutterite colony has many families living together on a large farm. It looks like a small village placed in the centre of farmland. There are **row houses**, which hold three or four families each. The church, community kitchen, and dining hall are near the homes. Farm buildings and animal pens are farther away. Hutterites farm grain crops, such as wheat, barley, oats, and canola.

The colony owns all property. It provides all members with food, clothing, housing, health care, and schooling. The group cares for each member from birth to death. Colonies grow their own food and make their own clothes. They build all of the buildings and care for the livestock, too.

Between 60 and 160 people live on each colony. When the colony becomes too large, it is divided in two. Half the group forms another colony on different land.

Hutterite girls learn to garden, cook, clean, and sew.

Hutterite communities have many row houses, a school and church, and a large kitchen in the *huf* (community yard).

Traditional Clothing

Hutterites wear the same type of clothing their ancestors wore. Boys and men wear **suspenders**, dark pants, a buttoned shirt, a dark coat, and a wide-brimmed, black hat. Married men grow a beard. Women wear long, printed dresses. All women wear their hair long. They cover their heads with black plaid or polka-dot **kerchiefs**. Young girls up to 10 years of age wear bonnets.

das Kopftuck
kerchief

das Kleid
dress

die Socken
socks

Think About It

What kinds of clothing do people from your culture wear? Do they wear it daily or only for special occasions?

Songs of Praise

Singing is an important part of Hutterite life. Most singing **praises** the Hutterite faith. Hutterites sing in church, in their homes, at festive occasions, and at other times. They know many songs from memory. Hutterites sing church **hymns** slowly. This is because the church service is restful and unhurried. Hutterites do not play musical instruments when they sing.

Some colonies have choirs that sing in hospitals or seniors' homes. Choirs often have ten to forty-five members. Most members are unmarried. They are often between 15 and 30 years of age. Choirs practise singing in the evening. Young people also sing together when they visit different colonies.

Table Rules

Here is part of a poem Hutterite children learn about table manners.

If a food is not prepared
The way you most would have it,
Do not speak up at once and say,
"I won't eat any of it."

You must not ask questions
About the food that's offered you,
And do not put your nose upon
The dishes passed before you.

Don't crunch things with your teeth
Or people will have fear
That wild beasts in the neighbourhood
Are coming very near.

Don't dip into the salt dish
Your little bit of food,
Nor put your fingers in it,
For that is very rude.

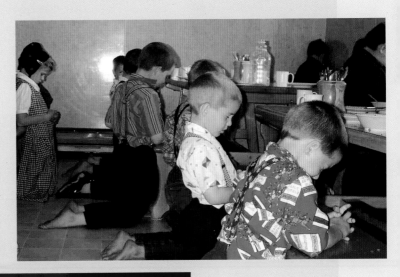

■ Hutterites say a prayer of thanks before eating a meal.

Think About It
What are some of the rules in your home?
Can you write a poem about them?

Farm Fresh Foods

For hundreds of years, Hutterites have grown all of their own food. They collect milk from their dairy cattle and eggs from their chickens. Their pigs, turkeys, and cattle give them meat. They grow vegetables in huge gardens on the colony.

The food served at mealtime is plain, healthy, and plentiful. There are special treats prepared when there is extra work, such as at harvest time. In the dining hall, women sit at long tables. Men sit on the opposite side of the room. Both men and women sit in order of their age and if they are married or single. Children eat in another room or building. There is little talk during mealtime.

One day's meals might include:

Breakfast: Bacon and eggs, bread and cheese, tea or coffee

Lunch: Fresh bread with jam, beef, potatoes, buttered beets, rice pudding

Supper: Fresh bread with cheese, baked beans, fried potatoes, hamburger, cold duck

Hutterites use pumpkin and squash to make many traditional recipes.

Women take turns cooking. Two women cook together for one week. The next week, two different women cook. This continues throughout the year.

16

Apple Cinnamon Loaf

With an adult's help, try making this simple apple cinnamon loaf using pancake or waffle mix.

Materials

1 large mixing bowl
1 smaller mixing bowl
electric mixer
loaf pan
rubber spatula
wooden spoon
125 millilitres butter or margarine
250 mL white sugar

2 eggs
5 mL vanilla
250 mL grated apple
500 mL pancake or waffle mix
5 mL baking powder
2 mL baking soda
2 mL salt
125 mL chopped walnuts
30 mL brown sugar
5 mL cinnamon

Preheat the oven to 180° Celsius.

In a large bowl, mix the butter, white sugar, and eggs. Beat with the electric mixer until smooth.

Stir the vanilla, grated apple, and walnuts into the mixture.

In the smaller bowl, stir the pancake mix, baking powder, baking soda, and salt.

Add the ingredients from the small bowl to the large bowl. Stir well.

Pour half the batter into a greased loaf pan.

Sprinkle half of the brown sugar and half of the cinnamon over the mixture.

Pour the remaining batter on top of the brown sugar and cinnamon.

Sprinkle the remaining cinnamon and brown sugar over the mixture.

With an adult's help, bake the mixture for 50 to 60 minutes. Remove from the pan 10 minutes after you take it from the oven. Let cool.

Serve warm, and enjoy.

Think About It

Think about the food your family eats during holiday meals. Does any of the food belong to a certain culture? With an adult's help, try making a special family recipe.

Cultural Contributions

Hutterites often sell **produce** from their farms at farmers' markets. People like to buy these fruits and vegetables because they are fresh. Onions, radishes, rhubarb, and pickled beans fill their booths. Hutterite women sometimes make quilts and pies to sell. Some men and boys make objects out of wood.

Hutterites carve toys from wood.

Boys take turns working in the carpenter's shop.

A Day in the Life

Here is what a day at a colony school might be like.

6:00 AM	Everyone wakes up and gets out of bed.
6:30 AM	The entire colony eats breakfast.
7:30 to 8:30 AM	A colony adult teaches German language and religion classes to the children.
8:50 AM	Children begin English school.
12:00 to 1:00 PM	The entire colony eats lunch together.
1:00 to 3:00 PM	English school continues.
3:00 PM	Girls clean the school building.
3:30 PM	Students do their German homework.
4:30 PM	School is finished for the day.
5:00 to 6:00 PM	Children do their chores.
6:00 to 7:00 PM	The entire colony attends church. They eat supper after the service.
7:00 PM	Children have 2 hours to complete their chores, do homework, and visit with family.
9:00 PM	Children prepare for bedtime.

Think About It

Think about your school day. Which things are the same as a Hutterite child's school day? Which things are different?

Hutterite children attend one- or two-room schools on the colony. Many grades share the classroom and teacher.

Further Research

How can I find more information about Hutterite culture?

- Libraries have many interesting books about Hutterites.

- The Internet offers some great Web sites dedicated to Hutterite colonies.

Where can I find a Web site to learn more about Hutterite culture?

Riverview Hutterite Colony School
www.sesd.sk.ca/grassroots/riverview/default.htm

The Hutterian Brethren
www.hutterites.org

St. John's-Ravenscourt School Grade 3 students visit the Sturgeon Creek Hutterite Colony
www.sjr.mb.ca/Jschool/JSNews/1999-00/G3Hutter/

How can I find more Web sites about Hutterites?

Using a search engine, such as yahoo.ca or google.ca, type in different search terms. Some terms you might try include "Hutterites," "brethren," and "colonies."

Hutterite children of all ages play together. Older children help and care for younger children.

Hearts, Flowers, and Dandy Designs

Materials

scissors
2 pieces of paper
coloured pencils

1. Cut one piece of paper so that it is square (21.5 centimetres by 21.5 cm).

2. Fold the square in half from corner to corner. This will form a triangle shape.

3. Fold the triangle in half.

4. Along one fold, draw half a heart.

5. Along the other fold, draw half a flower.

6. Keeping the paper folded, cut out the designs you drew.

7. Open up the paper and place it on the second piece of paper.

8. Trace the designs you cut out onto the paper below.

9. Remove the stencil and colour your designs.

Think About It

Does your culture make any special crafts? What kinds of designs do they use? Have you tried any of these crafts with your family?

What Have You Learned?

1

Why is this culture called Hutterites?

2

When did the first Hutterites come to Canada?

3

In which provinces do most Hutterites live?

4

Where do Hutterites eat their meals?

5

What languages do Hutterite children speak?

6	7	8	9	10
When do Hutterites begin to learn English?	How many hours do Hutterite children spend in classes each day?	At what age do boys and girls stop attending English school?	Do Hutterites buy their clothes in stores?	How many people usually live in a colony?

Answers

1. They are named after their first leader, Jakob Hutter. 2. 1918 3. Manitoba, Saskatchewan, and Alberta (the prairie provinces) 4. in a dining hall. The children eat separately from adults. The women sit on one side of the hall and the men sit on the other. 5. High German, Hutterite German, and English 6. They begin to learn English when they start school at age 5 or 6. 7. 8 hours 8. 15 or 16 years of age 9. No, they make their clothes at the colony. 10. between 60 and 160 people

Glossary

ancestors people from the past who are related to modern people

baptized people dipped into water as part of a ceremony to show their commitment to their church

colonies large farms where many families live

culture the customs, traditions, and values of a nation or people

dialect a different form of a language

harvest gathering of ripe fruits, vegetables, and grains

hymns religious songs

kerchiefs square pieces of fabric worn on the head or around the neck

praises worships

produce farmed food items, such as fruit and vegetables

row houses homes built side-by-side in a row to form one building

suspenders elastic straps worn over the shoulders to support pants

tradition cultural rituals, customs, and practices

Index

celebrations 8, 9
clothing 8, 12, 13, 23
colony 6, 7, 8, 9, 10, 11, 12, 14, 16, 19, 20, 23
cooking 12, 16
Czech Republic 4, 5

farmers' markets 18
farming 4, 6, 8, 9, 12, 18
food 8, 9, 12, 15, 16, 17

German 10, 11, 14, 19, 23

harvest 9, 16
housing 12
Hutter, Jakob 4, 23
hymns 14

language 7, 8, 10, 11, 19, 20, 22

meals 9, 15, 16, 17, 22
Moravia 4

North Dakota 6

religion 4, 8, 19

school 8, 10, 12, 19, 20, 23
South Dakota 4, 6, 7

World War I 4, 6